AROUND RUTLAND

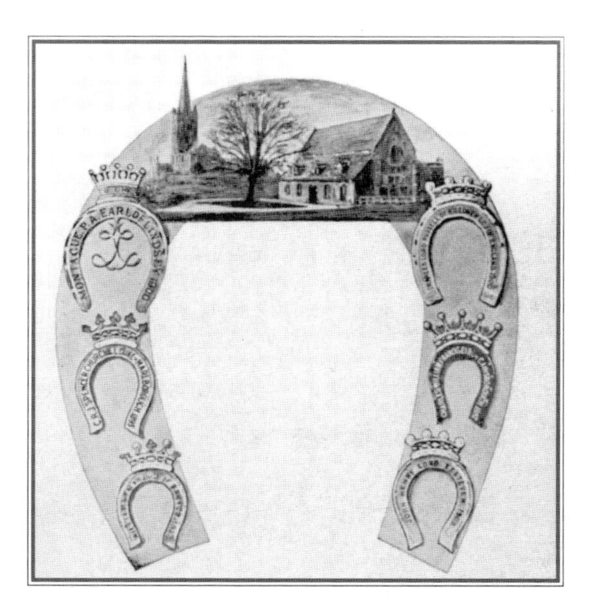

Oakham Church, Castle and six of the many horseshoes, forfeited by peers of the realm, that hang in the castle.

The lane from Ridlington, leading into Leighfield, 1985. This timeless scene represents a traveller's view of much of the network of minor roads that crisscross Rutland. Lanes that would appear to lead nowhere; but 'all roads lead to Oakham'! A line from G.K. Chesterton's poem, 'The Rolling English Road', could have been written with Rutland in mind: 'A reeling road, a rolling road, that rambles round the shire'.

BRITAIN IN OLD PHOTOGRAPHS

AROUND RUTLAND

TREVOR HICKMAN

SUTTON PUBLISHING LIMITED

Sutton Publishing Limited
Phoenix Mill · Far Thrupp · Stroud
Gloucestershire · GL5 2BU

First published 1996

Cover photographs: *front:* Market Overton, 1912; *back:* Horseshoes in Oakham Castle, 1920.

By the same author:
Around Melton Mowbray In Old Photographs
Melton Mowbray In Old Photographs
The Vale of Belvoir In Old Photographs
The History of Stilton Cheese

British Library Cataloguing in Publication Data
A catalogue record for this book is available from the British Library.

ISBN 0-7509-1174-3

Typeset in 10/12 Perpetua.
Typesetting and origination by
Alan Sutton Publishing Limited.
Printed in Great Britain by
Ebenezer Baylis, Worcester.

County boundary! The Rutland name-plate at Knob Bridge, that carries the Stapleford to Whissendine road across the famous Whissendine brook featured in many fox-hunting tales, viewed from below Hickman's Hill. Joseph Hickman farmed these fields at the end of the eighteenth century. The author is directly descended from this farmer, six generations removed. These name-plates were erected by Rutlanders who wished to retain their unique identity, much to the annoyance of some Leicestershire County Council Officers.

CONTENTS

In 1969 posters appeared all over Rutland bearing the words 'Don't Flood Rutland'. There was considerable opposition to constructing Empingham Reservoir, later to be named Rutland Water. Today very few people would be against this superbly landscaped expanse of water: it is a monument to twentieth-century civil engineering. Not only does it store much-needed water but it also provides marvellous leisure facilities and is a haven for wildlife. This photograph, taken from the Barnsdale Shore looking towards Edith Weston, shows a gaggle of Canada geese entering the water.

INTRODUCTION

This book has been compiled by an enthusiast for the county of Rutland and all it stands for; even though I have never lived in the county, the district around Oakham has been of interest to me for most of my life. I was born in Wymondham, a small village that is situated on the northern border of Rutland. My family has a long association and interest in Oakham; my mother worked at the local hospital and my great grandfather, Thomas Hickman, was a carrier operating into the town from Wymondham on market days in the 1890s. The district surrounding Oakham has been my playground for over fifty years, as I fished in the Melton to Oakham Canal as a child, cycled along the winding lanes and walked the footpaths and bridleways that crisscross the county. In later years I was associated with a number of publishing projects that resulted in the production of splendid books about the county. I am indebted to David Tew, John Barber and John Buchanan who introduced me to many new facets of this unique district through the books I published for them. A few years ago I was discussing the village of my birth with Eddie Hudson, the editor of the splendid independent local newspaper the *Rutland Times*, regarding my interest in Rutland and the fact that many people living in Wymondham visit Oakham, take an interest in its businesses, obtain medical services from a Rutland doctor, use the county hospital, purchase provisions in Oakham and send their children to school in the town. Eddie stated, 'Wymondham has always considered it should be involved in Rutland's affairs'; this of course is true!

In the late nineteenth and well into the twentieth century Wymondham was a postal district of Oakham. Many centuries before that the lords of the manor of Wymondham were the Berkeleys, some of whom were appointed sheriffs of the county of Rutland. They were related by marriage to the Ferrars family, who held the manor of Oakham after the Norman Conquest. Three Berkeleys were sheriffs: Thomas Berkeley in 1444 and 1473, Maurice Berkeley in 1489 and a second Maurice Berkeley in 1570. In addition to the lords of the manor most of the old-established families living in north-east Leicestershire and parts of Lincolnshire would have been involved in Rutland affairs, through trade and marriage, over many centuries, not least this one.

In this book I have selected photographs that have been extracted from the accumulation of illustrations and ephemera covering the district around Oakham that I have collected since I was a child. As a frequent visitor with a deep interest in exploring the county I have placed emphasis on roads through villages, the railway system and bridges crossing rivers and streams. In many ways this is a nostalgic collection. During the late 1940s I cycled around Rutland often on a Sunday afternoon with a group of friends. One journey still remains very clear: we rode on to the Great North Road at Tickencote, travelling north to Grantham, passing the old toll house at Woolfox, the ruined public house The Blue Bull near South Witham and on to Grantham, five abreast across the single-track highway, meeting two cars on the whole journey. This single-track road was still being used by horse-drawn vehicles, as the evidence of their passing created a hazard to cyclists. Many years later Rigby Graham and I walked along the towpath of the derelict Melton to Oakham Canal, a memorable but difficult journey commencing at The Boat Inn, Melton Mowbray, and finishing at The Odd House Inn at Oakham. The pair of us had a continuous fight with brambles and overgrown hawthorn hedges that endeavoured to block our path. In the 1950s I was also introduced to a unique feature of Rutland, Ruddles Ales. A pint of County has been my favourite tipple ever since.

The archaeology of the county has always interested me, and for a number of years I was part of Fred Adams' team on the rescue dig at Lower Hambleton prior to the site being covered by Rutland Water, and also on the medieval site at Whitwell. Recently I have been searching for the remains of the early bridges that span the rivers and streams of the county; to do this I have driven along many of the lanes in Rutland, encountering views that seem to have changed little in fifty years; but of course this is not true because open-cast mining has played its part in shaping the countryside and changing the views. Today all that remains in many instances are the low cliffs along the headlands of some fields and, of course, the gullets filled with water that now serve as fishing reserves; there is always Rutland water around the corner!

One feature of Rutland that is timeless is its churches. In the pages of this book I have reproduced some photographs of the stone carvings produced by the Norman stonemasons in the many places of worship nestling in the villages and hamlets of the county.

I have included a photograph from almost every parish as a tribute to the district's individuality and I trust this small book will find its place among the vast collection of books and

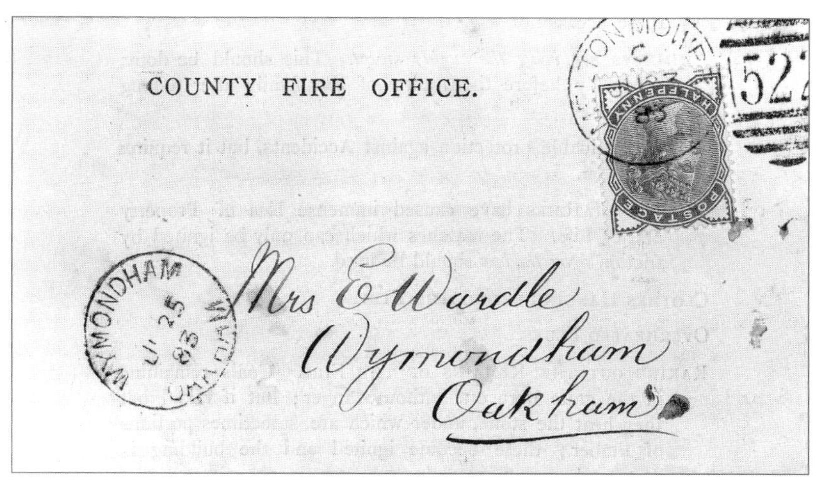

A letter that was posted at Melton Mowbray on 23 June 1883, taken to Oakham by train, then transferred to a local train for delivery to Whissendine station (named Wymondham Midland until 1878), to be collected by William Payne, the postmaster, who had walked across the fields from Wymondham. Finally it was franked, after a two-day journey, at the village post office.

pamphlets that have been published about Rutland over the last three hundred years. It is my contribution to the independent spirit of the people of Rutland. Since the county was formed some time in the twelfth century it has developed its own identity, which it has never lost. To some of us Rutland has always been there; at long last the bureaucrats accept this.

Thomas Fuller in his *History of the Worthies of England*, published in 1662, wrote: 'Let not the inhabitants of Rutland complain, that they are pinned up within the confines of a narrow county; seeing the goodness thereof equals any shire in England for fertility of ground: But rather let them thank God, who hath cast their lot into so pleasant a place, giving them a goodly heritage.' These words apply equally today; all we need to add is 'and an abundance of water'!

This book is presented to the reader by an interested outsider, looking in. It is how I see the district around Oakham, my favourite market town, and the county of Rutland as a whole. I take full responsibility for the presentation of the photographs and I trust the reader will enjoy this collection in the spirit that it is presented, as a record of a county that has 'much in little'.

A plan of the area covered in this book showing the names of the districts (hundreds) which have been chosen and used as main headings and the parishes featured within each section. This is adapted from the *Victoria History of the Counties of England*, Rutland edition (1908).

SECTION ONE

THE TOWN OF OAKHAM

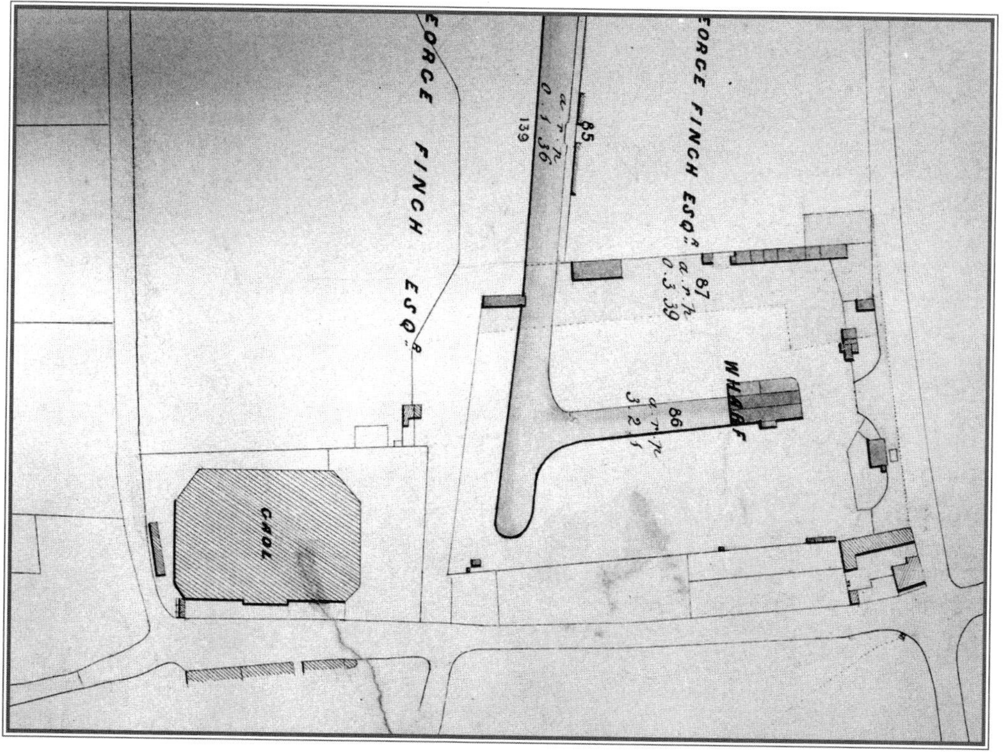

A plan of the wharf area of the Melton to Oakham Canal at the junction with Ashwell and Burley roads, drawn by Stephen Fry around the year 1850. The manager of the wharf was Thomas Salmon and The Boat Inn on Ashwell Road was run by Thomas Copeland. This canal opened through to Oakham in 1802, so enabling cheap coal to be retailed in the town. This brought about an immediate change in the quality of life of the inhabitants of Oakham, and opened up the district to trade with the industrial heartland of England. The county gaol was built in 1810 and held a treadwheel used as punishment for the prisoners committed to hard labour; according to records of the time executions 'on the drop' were few in number.

A bird's-eye view of Oakham, looking south from the tower of the Church of All Saints, 1905. To the right of the photograph runs Church Street; the thatched cottage on the corner with High Street is now the TSB.

Midland Railway station, Oakham, 1916. The station master was William George Wearn. In the right background in the station yard can be seen signs for A.M. Bradshaw, coal merchant, and also Ellis & Everard Ltd whose manager was Mr H. Toll. The cyclist standing nearest to the railway fence is George Samuel Dexter, coal dealer.

The polygonal butter cross with stocks in the Market Place, 1908. This is the traditional site of the weekly Monday market. The area has been very well preserved and has changed little in eighty-eight years. Oakham School House stands in the background.

The stocks that stand under the roof covering the butter cross, 1906. Why five holes? Two people could sit side by side on the steps of the market cross with their legs secured. Was it possible to secure five people by one leg after a busy day at the local courthouse?

The thatched cottage that stood on the corner of Church Street and High Street (see p. 10). Now, as the TSB, it is much altered.

Two Oakham shields. The shield on the right is that of Ferrers, Earl of Derby (argent six horseshoes gable), with seven nail holes in each shoe. These are the legendary Rutland horseshoes. The shield on the left, drawn by Rigby Graham, is a true Rutland horseshoe that came off a shire horse that pulled a plough in the fields around Pickworth. Unfortunately this drawing caused much controversy for the Rutland and District Sunday Football League, who displayed it on their letter headings, etc., in 1982.

Oakham Castle, 1769. This Norman hall was built by Walkelin de Ferrers *c.* 1190, and should correctly be described as a fortified manor house.

The fortified manor house known as Oakham Castle, *c.* 1908.

"Cross Keys" Inn, New St., Oakham.

A. C. GREEN,

BASKET 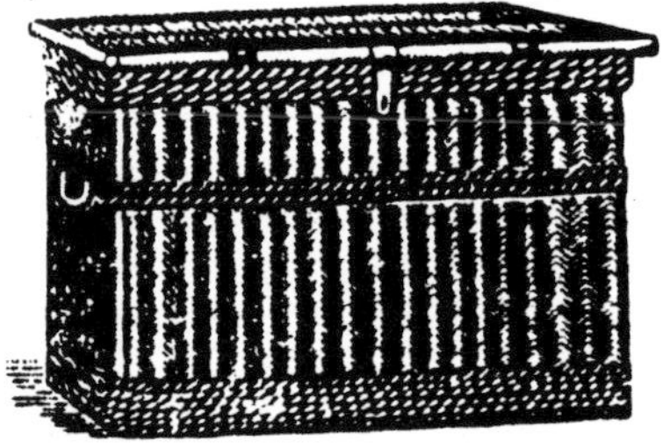 MAKER

All kinds of LINEN HAMPERS made and lined complete as above.

CLOTHES BASKETS, STABLE BASKETS, SCUTTLES, &c.
of every description, Made on the Premises.

CANE CHAIRS RE-SEATED.

REPAIRS PROMPTLY ATTENDED TO.

The advertisement of a well-known basket maker operating out of The Cross Keys Inn, New Street, in 1909. William Charles Green was the landlord of this public house.

High Street, 1918. The first shop on the left is Maud Baxter's baby linen shop, in the centre background stands Alfred Lenton's grocer's shop and to the right is The Crown Public House, licensee William Merriken.

High Street, 1906. In the centre background is August Fligge's boot and shoe shop. His speciality was boots and shoes made for the aristocracy. The prominent house on the left is Neville House; japonica still covers the wall.

R. DRAKE,

Saddle & Harness Maker

HIGH ST., OAKHAM.

All Kinds of Light and Heavy Harness, Horse Clothing, &c., &c., made to order.

Also keeps in Stock—Straps of all kinds, Fawn and Jute Rugs, Girths, Braces, Purses, Webs, Machine Belting, Shoe and Stable Brushes, &c., Bits, Spurs, Burnishers, Composite Harness Dye, Sponges, Wash Leathers, &c. Driving, Hunting, and Cart Whips.

All kinds of TRAVELLING BAGS to order. PORTMANTEAUS REPAIRED.

Special attention called to LEGGINGS of every kind and make.

Advertisement for a well-known harness maker, 1909.

The junction of Catmose Street and Stamford Road, *c.* 1918. On the left now stands Melton Lodge, built in 1927; on the right-hand corner plot stands the Rutland County Library. This is one of the most radically altered areas of Oakham.

Catmose Street, 1920. The Bell Inn on the right was run by Alfred Brown. It is long since demolished and the Rutland County Library occupies this area.

Rutland morris men dancing near the Market Place.

The Market Place in the 1920s.

Oakham School sanatorium and gardens, *c.* 1910. Before it became part of the school complex it was the vicarage; now it is College House. For information on the educational revolution that took place at Oakham School from 1958 onwards read *Operation Oakham* by John Buchanan, 1984.

The dining hall at Oakham School in the 1920s.

Wharfland, Oakham School in the 1920s.

The Quad, Oakham School in the 1920s. For further reading on this fine school the author recommends *The Story of Oakham School* by John Barber, 1983.

Catmose, 1904. This was the home of the Right Honourable Gerard James Noel, PC, DL, JP, and Lady Augusta Noel. Now it is the main offices of the Rutland District Council.

The Church of All Saints and the Old Grammar School, 1908. The Grammar School is now the Shakespeare Centre used by Oakham School, restored in 1969 with money donated by John Jerwood. In the foreground stands the remains of the defensive wall that surrounded Oakham Castle (see page 23).

The Melton to Oakham Canal at the edge of the Oakham School playing fields, 1983.

Springfield, Ashwell Road, the home of Lord Londonderry, 1910.

ROBT. HIBBINS

HAS A LARGE STOCK OF

First=class BOOTS & SHOES

OF EVERY DESCRIPTION.

Hunting, Shooting, Fishing, Cycling and Golf Boots made to order.

REPAIRS neatly and promptly executed.

MELTON ROAD, OAKHAM.

An advertisement for a shoe shop on Melton Road, 1909.

Melton Road, 1918. The first shop on the left is the retail area of John Robert Atton's bakery, the fourth shop along is Herbert Sharpe's confectionery. In the centre background is Oakham railway crossing with the gates open.

SECTION TWO

OAKHAM SOKE

The interior of Oakham Castle, 1893. Two town constables are in attendance prior to the quarter sessions being held in the hall. Much has been written about the famous Rutland horseshoes that peers of the realm are required to deposit at the castle when they visit the town. The origins of this ritual date back to the time of the Ferrars family who were lords of the manor at Oakham. This Norman family was granted vast areas of England after the conquest in 1066, and is credited with demanding horseshoes from visiting knights who arrived on horseback during the turbulent years of the twelfth century. There is some logic in this; if a horse loses one shoe it is not immobilized, but cannot travel very quickly: visiting nobles did sometimes attack their hosts. Take off a horseshoe and the rider loses considerable mobility. Visiting nobility became aware of the Ferrars' demand at Oakham and secured one of the four shoes with seven nails instead of eight. This allowed the forfeit shoe to be easily removed. These shoes were hung on nails and eventually nailed to the wall. As the countryside became more stable it became a ritual, not a safety precaution. The prongs of the Ferrars horseshoes hang down, in line with all farriers' shoes. The horseshoes of other noble houses were also displayed upside down, recording their luck at keeping out of the way of the Ferrars!

BELTON-IN-RUTLAND

The junction of Church Street with Chapel Street, *c*. 1914. The village war memorial now stands in front of the church gates.

The Church of St Peter, 1910. The vicar was George James Pattison. To the left stands the Old Hall.

The Baptist Chapel, 1910; erected in 1843, it could seat 120 people. The road to Loddington leads off to the left.

Thatched cottage, Belton, 1904. It is long since demolished. The photographer stood on the rising ground in Nether Street.

BRAUNSTON-IN-RUTLAND

The junction of Knossington Road and High Street, 1910. In the centre background is John Beadman's grocer's shop; he was also a beer retailer. The date stone inscribed P.B. 1860 is still retained on the wall. On the right is the wheelwright's shop of Horace Cunington.

An aerial view of The Old Plough public house, 1960. This famous inn was built as a posting house in the 1780s. Today it is a popular rendezvous for Rutlanders and visitors to the county. It serves fine food in the conservatory restaurant built at the rear of the premises.

The carved stone figure that stands near the west door of Braunston Church, representing a female with prominent breasts. It could be a pre-Roman pagan god of fertility. A similar carved stone named La Gran'mere stands in the churchyard in the parish of St Martin, Guernsey, dated 600 BC. Both carved stones show the influence of prehistoric menhir carving and Mediterranean sculpture work.

Thomas Heycock (1788–1862) of Braunston Manor, *c.* 1860. Tommy Heycock was a rough rider, a contemporary of the famous Dick Christian. They were friendly rivals, taking the high fences in their stride, in all the East Midlands fox-hunting counties.

The footbridge opposite the church. This stone bridge with cutwaters facing the flow of the River Gwash would have been used by packhorses when the river was in flood.

BROOKE

The Norman arch above the doorway to the Church of St Peter.

The packhorse bridge across the Gwash, possibly built by monks of the Augustine Priory in the fourteenth century. The small shelf above the stone arch would have supported a carving of the patron saint guarding the travellers using the bridge.

The coat of arms of the Noel, family (or fretty gules and a quarter ermine), who purchased the priory site in 1549 and built a large house nearby.

The sixteenth-century octagonal porter's house. This is all that remains of the great house built by the Noels; it was converted into a dovecote in the eighteenth century.

EGLETON

Thatched cottages on Main Street near the junction with Orchard Close, *c.* 1906. They were demolished in a road widening scheme.

Norman arch above the door of St Edmund's Church.

LANGHAM & BARLEY THORPE

The village pump standing on the wide grass verge in Well Street, 1904. The thatched cottages on the right have been demolished; only the brick cottage, No. 25 built in 1876, still stands near the church.

The Cottesmore Hounds at the Cold Overton, Langham crossroads, *c.* 1936. They are being led by Major C.C. 'Chetty' Hilton-Green.

Langham Brewery, *c.* 1900, when Henry Parry was owner and George Ruddle was manager. George Ruddle purchased the brewery in 1911 and it was run by the family until 1986 when it was purchased by Grand Metropolitan, then Courage. In 1992 it was taken over by Grölsch, the Dutch brewers.

A Ruddles dray outside the Church of St Peter and St Paul, Langham, 1966.

A temporary inflatable warehouse at the Langham Brewery site, 1978.

One of the finest beers in the world, brewed at Langham in the famous brewery. It is served in inns throughout the UK, and affords a pleasant surprise when it is encountered further afield at such public houses as The Devil's Hole, on the north coast of Jersey.

The bronze head of Jupiter now in the British Museum, found in 1890 by Sir A.W. Franks. This Roman artefact is presumed to have come from the Roman villa at Ranksborough Hill, to the west of the present village.

T. O. ROUSE,

Bird & Animal Preserver

Langham, near Oakham.

An advertisement for the local taxidermist Thomas Oldham Rouse, who was also a farmer in the village, 1909.

Ranksborough Hall, 1916, the home of the Lord Lieutenant of the County of Rutland, Major-General Lord, CB, CVO.

DAVID TIDD,

Grocer, Provision Dealer & Tobacconist,

LANGHAM, near Oakham, Rutland.

AGENT FOR "ONE-AND-ALL" SEEDS.

MAZAWATTEE TEA, 1/6, 1/8, 1/10, 2/- GOMETTA, 2/-

PERFECTION, 1/6, 1/8, 1/10, 2/- RENOWNED, 1/6, 1/8, 1/10, 2/-

Advertisement for a popular local grocer, 1909.

Pat Wolfe behind the bar at The Black Horse public house with her two assistants, Barbara Denny and Helen Secret, 1969. On the counter stand the two famous jugs: Pat served her ale direct from the barrel into the jugs, then into her customer's glass.

Barleythorpe Hall, 1916, the home of the Earl of Lonsdale, DL, JP, described in the House of Commons as 'almost an Emperor and not quite a gentleman'!

Lord Lonsdale with his private pack of hounds that he bred and raised at Barleythorpe Hall. The Yellow Earl was elected MFH of the Cottesmore in 1907 and resigned in 1911. A man larger than life, his carriages and cars were all painted yellow. He founded the Automobile Association, hence their yellow livery, and was the man behind the famous boxing trophy, the Lonsdale Belt.

LEIGHFIELD

A Second World War 'pillbox' standing proudly on top of a hill near Leighfield Farm.

The rolling hills of Leighfield, a parish without a village! Leighfield Forest was subject to disafforestation *c.* 1630; it was then enclosed and became rich grazing land. It was an area for Stilton cheese production in the eighteenth century. The Neville family held the property from the middle of the twelfth century to the end of the fourteenth century. (Their arms are azure cruisilly with three fleurs de lis coming out of leopards' heads argent.) In the middle of the fifteenth century it came into the possession of the Hastings, then in turn the Noel, the Digby and the Finch family.

CLIPSHAM

Clipsham Hall, 1904, the home of John William Handley Davenport-Handley, DL, JP.

The gates to Yew Tree Avenue, 1922. This avenue of superb topiary is now maintained by the Forestry Commission. It is a haven for wildlife: orchids grow in the grass verges and deer roam across the driveway. Originally the driveway to Clipsham Hall, the clipping of these yew trees to their amazing shapes commenced in 1870, under the direction of Amos Alexander, head forester to the estate.

Cutting stone in the quarry at Clipsham in 1948, for use in the restoration programme at the House of Commons, owing to bomb damage in the Second World War. Note 'H.C.' painted on the stone blocks. These famous quarries had been worked since the twelfth century, supplying stone for building the cathedrals of Ely and Peterborough, colleges at Oxford and numerous village churches.

Clipsham stone quarry, 'The Big Pits', 1947. No blasting ever took place in these quarries: drilling and driving in wooden wedges was the main method of extracting the large blocks of stone.

WHITWELL

A general view of Whitwell, *c.* 1910.

The foundations of a Roman villa excavated in 1976 at Whitwell, when the car park for the fishing lodge at Rutland Water was being constructed.

SECTION THREE

ALSTOE

Alstoe Mount, 1983. A motte and bailey fortress to the north-east of Burley-on-the-Hill. The hundred court for Alstoe district would have been held here, possibly as early as the thirteenth century.

ASHWELL

A general view of the village from Braeside off Cottesmore Road, 1906. The Primitive Methodist Chapel was built in the gardens on the right in 1915.

Ashwell church fête, 26 July 1991, with Dora Barber drawing a tombola ticket and her sister Flo waiting to pay for one.

Ashwell Hall, 1902. This hall was built in 1879 by Westley Richards, the famous gun maker.

Colonel F.G. Blair of Ashwell Hall, 1902. Colonel of the Leicestershire Yeomanry, he served in the Boer War, was wounded, mentioned in dispatches, awarded the South African medal and made a Companion of the Bath. He was also High Sheriff of Rutland in 1886.

Gatekeeper's cottage, Langham Road, serving Ashwell crossing on the Nottingham to Peterborough railway line, *c.* 1920. It is long since demolished: all that remains is the outside privy.

The end of the hunt: the Cottesmore hounds close in on a fox in a stubble field near the derelict Melton to Oakham Canal, Ashwell. The huntsman (left) is Neil Coleman.

BURLEY-ON-THE-HILL

The south-facing view of Burley House, 1904, the home of the Rt. Hon. George Henry Finch, MP, JP. This famous house has been converted into seven units, fine country houses, by Kit Martin, a property developer who specializes in converting large stately houses into smaller properties.

On 6 August 1908, Burley House was gutted by fire. This photograph shows the Melton Mowbray horse-drawn fire engine standing in front of the main entrance; such appliances would have made little or no difference to the eventual outcome of such a disaster.

This canal mile post was originally sited on the tow-path of the Melton to Oakham canal at Turn overbridge near the Cottesmore hunt kennels. It was removed during a road widening scheme and stood in the front garden of a farm house at Burley-on-the-Hill for many years; in 1984 it was purchased by the author and David Tew, who then presented it to the Rutland County Museum, where it resides today. For further information on the canal that connected Melton Mowbray with Oakham consult *The Melton to Oakham Canal* by David Tew, 1984.

The Hermitage, Burley Wood, 1930. This summer house, constructed from tree trunks and branches, and thatched with reeds from Burley fish ponds, was burnt down in 1960.

The Forge, Burley-on-the-Hill, 1909. William Chambers is fitting a shoe to a pony.

"UNDER A SPREADING CHESTNUT TREE, THE VILLAGE SMITY STANDS."

WM. CHAMBERS,

SHOEING FORGE for HUNTERS

BURLEY-ON-THE-HILL, near OAKHAM,

William Chambers' advertisement, 1909, carrying the legend taken from Longfellow's poem 'The Village Blacksmith'. Henry Wadsworth Longfellow (1807–82), the American poet, is said by many historians to have gained inspiration from the romantic setting on the hill at Burley.

COTTESMORE & BARROW

Main Street, Cottesmore, 1904. The church gates are on the right; the village fish and chip shop now stands on the left.

The Leas, Cottesmore, 1904. The Sun public house (landlord Richard Thomas Benstead) stands on the left. The thatched cottage on the right has been demolished and is now Bland's Bus servicing area.

The Sun public house, 1940. The car UP 5560 was owned by Reg Bland who lived in the cottage opposite.

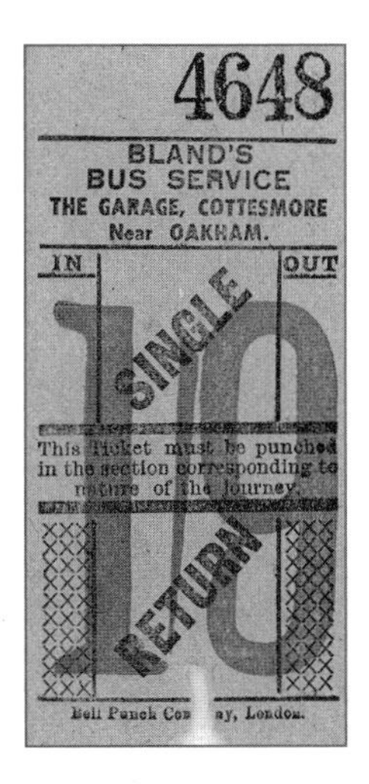

A 1*s* 9*d* bus ticket issued by Bland's Bus Service.

Ivy Bland in the early 1960s. Ivy and Reg Bland ran their local bus service from Cottesmore during the dark days of the Second World War through the villages around Oakham and on to Melton Mowbray. The author has fond memories of using this bus with his parents on market days during the war and later in the 1950s. Crates containing poultry were packed on top of the bus and excess luggage was stored in the cavernous boot. Ivy's cheerful greeting and friendly approach was appreciated by all who knew her: nothing was ever too much trouble for her. Bland's Bus Service, started by Reg Bland in 1929, still operates around Oakham.

A ruined administrative building standing on the site of Cottesmore Wharf, 1968. It serviced the Melton to Oakham Canal, but is long since demolished.

The sheep dyke, *c.* 1920, now filled in. Rose Cottage stands in the left background.

A line of Fairey Battles at Cottesmore, 1939. These planes formed part of 35 Squadron. Work on the construction of Cottesmore airfield began in 1935. It became a strategic base during the Second World War and has played a very important part in the defence of the British Isles ever since. For further information on this airfield consult *The History of Royal Airforce Cottesmore* by Norman Roberson and Jack Talliss, 1991.

One of the Tornadoes of the Tri-National Tornado Training Establishment (TTTE) coming in to land. This three-nations training programme involving Great Britain, Germany and Italy was started in April 1978.

The base of the medieval market cross that still stands in the centre of the small village of Barrow.

The Wide Hole, Barrow, on the Melton to Oakham Canal, 1968. Possibly constructed as a reservoir, this expanse of water on the derelict canal is now a haven for wildlife. Market Overton wharf can be seen in the background.

EXTON

Stamford Road, 14 June 1932.

Top Street and the market square, *c.* 1910.

Fort Henry, a summer house built in 1785, to a design by the Stamford architect William Legg. In the 1950s extensive quarrying took place near the lake in front of this building: see *Sundew in Rutland* by Alan Winterton, 1995. In the background stands the 'Bark Temple'.

The ruins of Exton Hall, 1910. This hall had been burnt down in 1810 and a new hall built in 1851.

GREETHAM

A view of the houses off Pond Lane, *c.* 1910. A road improvement programme is taking place, and mounds of crushed stone lie in front of the site of the old village pond.

The Ram Jam Inn and Garage on the Great North Road, near Stretton, 1928, prior to the major rebuilding programme that commenced in that year. This is a record of the transition of horse-drawn vehicles to motor vehicles: the garage has a water pump still in the forecourt for use by coach drivers, providing refreshment to horses and passengers alike.

Left: The Ram Jam Inn after restoration, *c*. 1940. The sign above the door is misleading, and has rude connotations. The name is derived from a drink, a type of punch that was bottled and sold at this inn in the late eighteenth century. Right: The bar at this famous 'roadhouse' on the Great North Road, *c*. 1930. Between the years 1928 and 1950 it was a very comfortable hotel; it then entered into a period of decline. Today it is a fine hostelry, part of Hart Hambleton plc. In this photograph a collection of prize-fighting prints are visible on the east wall, recording the fight at Thistleton Gap (see p. 63) a few miles to the north-west of the hotel.

The tennis court that was built in the disused stone quarry on the north side of the hotel, *c*. 1930. In the background can be seen the Great North Road (A1) defined with a line of young trees.

MARKET OVERTON

Main Street, 1904, looking south. The cottage in the centre background is being re-thatched. The Hall, the home of the Misses Wingfield, is on the right; on the left is Market Overton House.

Main Street, 1904, looking north. The forge is in the left background (William Burnsnall, blacksmith).

Presentation evening at The Three Horse Shoes Inn, December 1993. From left to right: Charles Wilson (landlord), Brian Embry (Chairman of the Royal Leicestershire and Rutland Wycliffe Society for the Blind), Neville Stafford (auctioneer). The cup was presented to this public house for raising the most money for the society during the year.

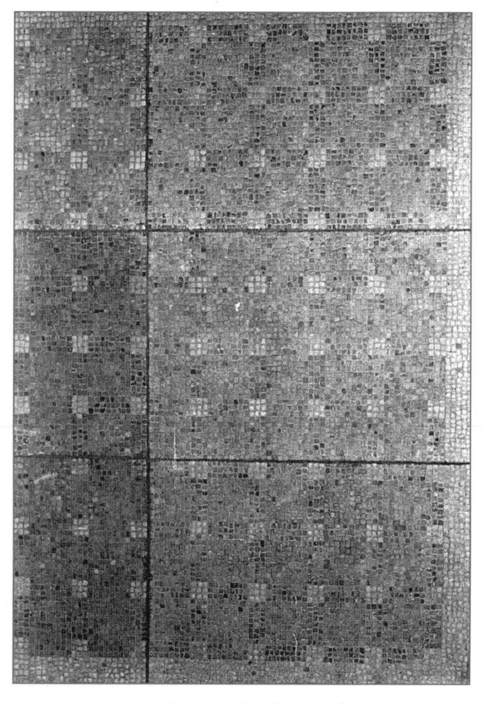

Left: A Roman steelyard and pot excavated at the ironstone quarry to the north of the village in 1935. Right: A Roman tessellated pavement (*c.* AD 350) unearthed during quarrying operations by Stewarts and Lloyds Mining Co., April 1960. The floor of the main room of a Romano-British house, made up of cut segments of roof tiles, local stone and hard stone from Huntingdonshire, this complete pavement is now on display at the British Steel Offices in Corby.

The village stocks with the forge in the background, 1912, when Herbert Skins was blacksmith. This building is now used as a surgery by the local doctor, and known as 'The Old Forge Surgery'.

A Berry shovel operating in the ironstone quarry near Woodwell Head, 1935.

STRETTON

Main Street, Stretton, 1916. The carrier's cart is being unloaded outside the entrance to The White Horse public house (landlord William Todd). Deliveries of mail were made from this cart to the post office opposite, which was run by Miss Elizabeth Elson.

The Jackson Stops (The White Horse). For many years prior to the 1950s this public house, then The White Horse, was up for sale through Jackson Stops, a London-based estate agent. The White Horse sign fell down, so the only name visible was the agent's sign board, and by popular demand this public house was re-named.

The landlord of the Jackson Stops public house collecting pennies from the nurdling drawer. The world championships of this public house game are played annually in this bar. Players start with thirteen old pennies each, and throw them from a distance of seven feet into a hole three inches in diameter on a bench with a lead 'splash back'. Each player throws his pennies in turn; the winner is the first person to score thirteen.

The Cottesmore Hunt at Stocken Hall, 1904 (MFH Evan Hanbury). Stocken Hall was the home of Captain Philip Francis Tillard, RN, and Lady Francis Cecil Tillard. Captain Tillard was appointed Commander of the Royal Yacht *Victoria and Albert* in 1888. He commanded HMS *Dido* during the Boxer Rebellion, off Beijing and the north China coast, 1900–1901.

TEIGH

The interior of the Church of the Holy Trinity, 1925. The vicar was Revd Simon Gee.

The thanksgiving plate fixed in Teigh Church recording that every person who served in the First World War from the village returned safely to their families. Teigh is one of the few 'Thankful Villages' in England where every person who served returned.

THISTLETON

The main road through the village, *c.* 1936. On the right is Church View Cottage, built in 1863, and Church Cottage, built in 1851; centre background stands Grange Farm.

An engraving published in 1812 recording the famous fight that took place near Thistleton Gap on 28 September 1811. This was the first defence of the heavyweight boxing championship of the world between Tom Cribb of England and Tom Molineux of America. Cribb was declared the winner after eleven rounds, lasting nineteen minutes ten seconds. For further information concerning this bare fist contest, read *Tom Cribb at Thistleton Gap* by Dennis Prestidge, 1971.

WHISSENDINE

Ashwell Road, *c.* 1905. On the left is the Primitive Methodist Church, built in 1868; opposite, on the right, is the road to Wymondham.

Whissendine windmill putting up a new sail *c.* 1900, when the miller was Thomas Hayes. For further information consult *Leicestershire and Rutland Windmills* by Nigel Moon, 1981. Nigel now owns this windmill and produces excellent flour for making into organic unbleached white bread at Paul's Bakery, Melton Mowbray.

Stapleford Road *c.* 1916. On the right, next to Harborough Cottage, stands South Lodge.

Harborough Cottage, Stapleford Road, 1925, the home of Benjamin Horne. In a wood called Cottage Plantation in nearby Stapleford Park, the sixth and last Earl of Harborough built a house for his mistress; when he died in 1859 his wife, Lady Harborough, gave instructions that the cottage should be demolished and rebuilt on land she owned at Whissendine, so allowing this 'Lady' to live in comfort for the rest of her life.

A view of the village of Whissendine from the tower of the Church of St Andrew, 1904. This photograph was taken by William Ashwell, organist at St Andrew's who was also an accountant, coal merchant, rate collector, photographer and insurance agent for the village.

The post office, Whissendine, 1904. Sub-postmaster Isaac Grocock was also the local draper and grocer.

Section Four

Martingsley

An engraving of Martingthorpe House, 1684. This fine house must have dominated the small village that by 1522 had almost disappeared. Today all that is left is the deserted house, Old Hall Farm. It was from this village that the name Martingsley Hundred is derived.

AYSTON

The crossroads at Ayston, *c.* 1910, a view that has changed little in eighty years.

The village green leading to the Church of St Mary.

EDITH WESTON

The village square, *c.* 1905. The photograph shows the west side of Well Cross; Alamanda Cottage is on the left.

The community pump that served many houses in the village, *c.* 1904. This pump has been removed and the village market cross that stood on the north side of the village square has been positioned on top of the well, and now carries the inscription EIIR 1952–1977!

A group of children standing in the village square, 1916. Centre right stands the post office (sub-postmaster Charles Bond).

A fine collection of seventeenth-century box tombs built just outside the main door to the Church of St Mary.

HAMBLETON & MIDDLE HAMBLETON

The Finch Arms public house, 1916 (landlord Edward Ireland).

The Cottesmore Hunt at Hambleton Hall, now one of the finest country house hotels in the British Isles. The high standard of service is maintained under the direction of the proprietor, Tim Hart.

The Priest's House, 1935. This late sixteenth-century building is fairly certain to have been an Elizabethan parsonage.

Old Hall, Middle Hambleton, 1977. Rutland Water has just covered Lower Hambleton and a tree planting programme has commenced.

LYNDON

The post office on Post Office Lane, 1925 (Noel Trengrove Rayson, sub-postmaster); centre background stands Beech House.

Lyndon Hall, 1935, the home of Roger John Edward Conant, JP.

MANTON & MARTINSTHORPE

Manton Midland Railway station, *c.* 1935. This station was sited at the southern end of Manton tunnel (in the middle distance) and was a junction for trains travelling to and from Oakham, Kettering and Peterborough. It opened on 1 May 1848 and closed 6 June 1966.

Manton Hall, 1910, the home of Robert Heathcote, JP.

Henry Finch, MA, JP, 1902. Resident of The Croft, he was Chairman of Oakham District Council and secretary to the Cottesmore Hunt.

The ruins of St Martin's Chapel, Martinsthorpe, *c.* 1930, prior to demolition. Old Hall Farm stands to the left. For further information on Martinsthorpe consult *A Celebration of Rutland*, 1994.

NORMANTON

The dining room block, Normanton House, 1916. The home of Evelyn, Dowager Countess of Ancaster, this fine building stood in a park of 400 acres well stocked with deer. It was demolished in 1925 by Tommy Crumbie, and a considerable amount of the faced stone was used in building The White House public house at Scraptoft, near Leicester.

The western portico of Normanton Church, 1935. These are the remains of a Georgian church built by the Heathcote family in 1765 and partially demolished in 1911. Now it 'floats' in Rutland Water.

PRESTON

The Manor House, 1904. This fine Jacobean house, the home of John Parker, was built *c.* 1600.

The grassed area at the end of Main Street, *c.* 1930. To the left stands Bay House, in the centre Lodge Cottage and to the right Wings House.

Preston windmill standing in the fields to the west of the village, *c.* 1916, when John Scott was the miller and local baker.

RIDLINGTON

Main Street, *c.* 1905. On the left stands the village school, built in 1873. On the right is Jotry Cottage, now no longer thatched; the first cottage on the right still retains its thatched roof, though in a different style.

Thatched cottage on Church Lane, *c.* 1905, displaying the date stone CIR 1776.

UPPINGHAM

The junction with Station Road, taken from South View, *c.* 1905.

Market Place, 1916. The Church of St Peter and St Paul (held by the Venerable Edward Marshain Moore, MA, Archdeacon of Oakham) dominates the square.

An auctioneer selling pigs at the annual fatstock show that takes place in November in the Market Place, Uppingham.

A general view of the town from London Road, *c.* 1935, looking north.

The new quadrangle of Uppingham School, 1930. This open area was created by demolishing cottages in School Lane during the years 1928 and 1929. For further information concerning this excellent school, consult *By God's Grace* by Bryan Matthews, 1984.

Meadhurst, 1925. This house on Ayston Road was purchased by Mr C.R. Haines in 1895, who extended it and gave it its present name, adding it to the existing two houses that were part of Uppingham School.

Uppingham windmill, Leicester Road, *c.* 1900. It is presumed that it ceased working in the 1890s. John Wadd was possibly the last miller. It was demolished during the years 1911 and 1912. The base of this old mill was uncovered during the excavations for the new Cavell Science Wing at Uppingham School in 1966.

Uppingham station, 11 June 1960. The Ivatt Class 2 MT 2–6–2 Uppingham to Seaton train is departing on the last day of passenger train operations. This station opened in September 1894 and finally closed in May 1964.

WARDLEY

The Church of St Botolph (vicar Revd David Michael Evans, BA), 1935. Some of the cottages that stand to the right of the church have been demolished.

The community pump that still stands in front of a cottage visible to the right of the church in the above photograph. This pump provided water for cattle and sheep secured in the nearby pinfold.

WING

Trimming ivy on the walls of The Small House, 8 Church Street, 1904. In the background stands the Church of St Peter and St Paul (vicar Revd Richard Allen White, MA).

The turf maze. Possibly constructed well over one thousand years ago, it is thought to have connections with a pagan ritual. There is a local tradition that people who were guilty of various religious misdemeanours were obliged to grovel round it on their knees as a penance.

Wing windmill at Weldon near Corby, Northamptonshire, *c.* 1900. Possibly purchased by Philip Hinckley in the early 1840s it was transported from Wing to Weldon some years later, where it ground corn for many years, going out of use during the early years of the First World War. It was blown down during a gale on Boxing Day 1915.

Jubilee Class 4–6–0 'Punjab' Down train to St Pancras leaving Glaston tunnel for Wing in 1955, pulling five carriages and a guards van.

SECTION FIVE

WRANDIKE

Wakerley Bridge, an important crossing of the River Welland. It was built as a packhorse bridge in the 1350s to serve the large market at Barrowden, connecting Wrandike district with Northamptonshire. In 1793 it was repaired and widened on the instructions of Henry Cecil, 10th Earl of Exeter, as clearly indicated on an engraved stone built into the lee side of the bridge. Evidence of two distinct styles of construction are visible. It is presumed that Henry Cecil paid for his half, Northamptonshire finance being raised for the remainder.

BARROWDEN

The Exeter Arms public house off the village green, Barrowden, 1953.

Boating on the River Welland, 1904. The Church of St Peter is in the background (vicar Revd Arthur Edward Hutchings).

The same three people as shown in the previous photograph, now posing in front of the Barrowden water mill, 1904. Henry Dixon was the miller and the local baker. This mill has been demolished and the area of the mill site has been 'landscaped'.

A cutwater on Wakerley Bridge, showing the eighteenth-century extension and a re-sited fourteenth-century carving of a saint, who continues to face the flow of the river.

BISBROOKE

The Gate Inn, 1936. Fred Barnett, publican and farmer, stands with his pony and trap at the main entrance.

Laundry Cottage, No. 7 Glaston Road, 1936.

CALDECOTT

The village green, 1936. The Plough public house (landlord Arthur Henry Musk) stands behind the yew-tree on the left.

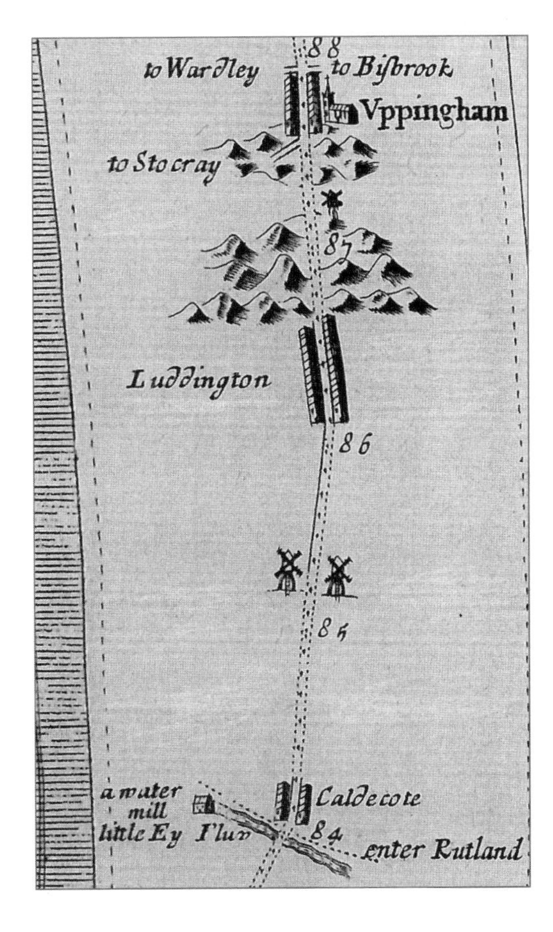

A detail from the 1675 strip map of the road from London to Oakham entering Rutland at Caldecott. These maps were drawn for use by travellers on horseback. The two windmills on the road from Caldecott to Lyddington eighty-five miles north of London must have been a welcome sight for many travellers using this road through the unfenced open fields to the south of the county. Lyddington is shown as an important village much larger than Uppingham!

GLASTON

The High Street (the A47) that runs through Glaston, 1936, looking west. The monkey puzzle tree standing on the left is now much higher. The entrance to Church Lane is on the right.

A view of the Church of St Andrew, 1936, obstructed by trees with the rectory on the left (vicar Revd John Henry Woods, MA).

The interior of the Church of St Andrew, 1935.

Jubilee Class 4–6–0 'Hood', Sheffield to St Pancras express, passing under the Seaton to Morcott Road bridge after leaving the Glaston tunnel, 3 October 1960.

LYDDINGTON

One of the occupants standing in the walkway at the side of the Bede House almshouse, *c.* 1905.

The main hall of Bede House, 1935. This almshouse was converted from the medieval bishop's palace in 1602 by Thomas Cecil, 1st Earl of Exeter. The bishop's palace was originally erected by Bishops Russell and Smith during the years 1480 to 1514.

The polygonal watch tower, part of the bishop's palace complex, 1916. The Church of St Andrew stands in the background (vicar Revd Spencer Richards Pocock, Th. Assoc., KC).

The Exeter Arms sign featuring David, Lord Burghley, 6th Marquess of Exeter, who was an international hurdler between the years 1924 and 1933. At the 1928 Olympic Games he won the gold medal, to be followed by a silver medal in 1932.

J. CHALLENDER,

HORSE BREAKER

"Exeter's Arms," LYDDINGTON, Uppingham.

Horses Broken to Single and Double Harness on reasonable terms

AT OWNER'S RISK.

Advertisement for John Challender's horse-breaking business, 1909. He was also the landlord of The Exeter Arms.

MORCOTT

Hens foraging on the Main Street of Morcott, 1910. The Church of St Mary stands in the middle distance (vicar Revd Brabazon Chambre Hallowes, MA).

The Baptist chapel, 1905. Originally built in 1710, it was extensively altered – virtually being rebuilt – in 1903 at the cost of £650.

Ivatt Class 2 MT 2–6–2 tank engine leaving Morcott tunnel *en route* for Seaton and Stamford, 24 October 1964.

The remains of Morcott windmill, 1964. This mill was rebuilt in 1968.

Laxton Lane packhorse bridge crossing the River Welland, carrying the bridleway from Morcott to Laxton in Northamptonshire. Used by horses and farm vehicles, it is an historic bridge that has suffered badly at the hands of the county councils concerned, who have cared little for its history when they 'repaired' the structure.

NORTH LUFFENHAM

The junction of Lyndon Road, Church Street and Pinfold Lane, 1904. The Fox and Hounds public house is on the left (landlord Thomas Henry Herbert).

The entrance to The Horse and Panniers inn, 1904. The licensee was Richard Chapman who was also the local baker, transporting bread around the lanes of Rutland by packhorse, maintaining the tradition set by previous landlords who were also bakers.

Community spirit is strong in most rural areas, but none more so than in Rutland. In this photograph, members of the North Luffenham Good Companions Club are about to board a community bus for one of their social outings, January 1993.

A surface-to-air missile standing outside the entrance to RAF North Luffenham.

PILTON

A display of horseshoes on the wall of the stable block, near the parish church, at the rear of the farmhouse built by Henry Shelton in 1823. Most of these horseshoes have an even number of holes, but some have an odd number, which was necessary when the hoof had split and it was not possible to secure the metal shoe with evenly spaced nails.

Pilton ironstone quarry, 1919. A steam shovel is loading two foot gauge wagons, pulled by a Bagnall engine, 'Pixie'. This engine was purchased by the late Revd Teddy Boston, 'The Vicar of Steam', and is now the main attraction at the Cadeby Light Railway Centre near Market Bosworth.

SEATON

The Main Street, 1923. The stone cottages on the left were built by Edward Philip Monckton, Lord of the Manor in 1881.

Seaton windmill, 1874. Josiah Royce was the miller.

Seaton junction and railway station, 28 August 1960. The 2.56 p.m. Ivatt Class 2 MT 2–6–2 for Uppingham is just leaving, with the push-pull train for Stamford parked in the sidings on the right. This station opened on 1 October 1894 and closed on 6 June 1966.

A Jubilee class 4-6-0 thundering across the famous Seaton Viaduct that spans the Welland Valley, *c.* 1955. Construction commenced on the structure in 1876, and it was opened to goods traffic two years later. It is Britain's longest brick-built viaduct: fifteen million bricks were used in its construction.

SOUTH LUFFENHAM

A view of the village from in front of the village church, *c.* 1905. In the middle distance stands Vine Farm, now The Grange.

The village centre, 1925. The Boot and Shoe Inn is on the left (landlord John Arthur Hunt), to the right is Mrs Sarah Elizabeth Chapman's shop and in the middle distance stands the Church of St Mary (vicar Revd John Francis Richards, MA).

A view of the village from Pinfold Lane, *c.* 1925. The village post office is now located in the farm buildings, in the centre of the photograph.

The Seaton to Stamford push-pull train at South Luffenham, 19 September 1956.

STOKE DRY

Top left: Entrance to the late Tudor north porch of the Church of St Andrew, *c.* 1905. Over this porch is a small 'priest's room'. Local legend has it that Sir Everard Digby, who lived at Stoke Dry, hatched the Gunpowder Plot with Guy Fawkes in this small room. They were both hanged, drawn and quartered in 1606. Top right: One of the interesting columns in the north chancel of Stoke Dry Church. A visit to this delightful church reveals much Norman carving, as well as fifteenth-century bench ends and unusual medieval wall paintings. Left: Stoke Dry rectory, 1904 – the home of Revd George Thurston, MA, vicar of St Andrews.

TIXOVER

The small village of Tixover sits in a broad valley to the north of the River Welland. Its church stands in the fields, indicating the site of a much earlier village. This cast-iron parish boundary marker is set centrally into the stone of Tixover bridge that spans the Welland at Duddington; to the right is Tixover in Rutland, to the left Duddington in Northamptonshire.

The Tixover–Duddington packhorse bridge viewed from Duddington water mill. A much altered bridge that once carried the busy A47 road, today it is a quiet backwater. The ancient cutwaters face the flow of the River Welland, as they have done for centuries.

SECTION SIX

EAST

Church bridge on the Oakham to Stamford Road at Empingham, the main highway connecting the east of the county with the county town. Built as a packhorse bridge, it has been repaired and altered many times. It was severely damaged in 1810 and 1880 when floods swept sections of the structure away, though some attempt has been made to retain the medieval cutwaters on the west side. They are not required today as the dam retaining Rutland Water is only a short distance further west and now controls the River Gwash.

EMPINGHAM

Church Street, 1936. The Church of St Peter is in the middle distance (vicar Revd Edward Ernest Law, BA).

Oakham Road, Empingham, *c.* 1940.

A disused water mill on the River Gwash at Empingham, *c.* 1905. Charles Speed was listed as the miller and farmer using this mill in 1877.

The war memorial to the parishioners of Empingham who were killed during the First World War, unveiled 11 November 1920.

Church bridge, 1936. 'Brian and Rene' are sitting on the parapet. In 1958 this parapet was removed and the roadway widened from thirteen feet to sixty feet.

ESSENDINE

The Norman tympanum (*c.* 1140) above the south doorway of St Mary's Church.

Class A4 streamlined Pacific No. 4468 *Mallard* entering Essendine station, 9 September 1948. It was on the 'Essendine Straight' that *Mallard* achieved the highest speed of any steam engine – 126 m.p.h. – on 3 July 1938. This world record has never been broken. The station opened on 1 August 1852 and closed on 15 June 1959.

GREAT CASTERTON

The Rectory, 1904 – the home of Revd John Scott Ramsey, MA, vicar of the Church of St Peter and St Paul.

The Norman font in the Church of St Peter and St Paul.

An engraved bronze plaque of a Roman goddess (*c.* AD 400) found at Great Casterton during the excavations that commenced in 1959. A large Roman town was built here during the first century AD which was continually occupied until Saxon times. Romano-Saxon pottery has been uncovered, along with evidence of attacks by Danish invaders in 867–76.

The bases of Roman pillars uncovered at the site of a villa during the 1959 excavations.

One of the most important discoveries in any excavation in Rutland was made in a clay pit at Great Casterton on 19 June 1968, when an excavator driver uncovered a pile of fossil bones. These bones were stacked and later collected by staff of Leicester Museums. On analysis they proved to be the remains of a cetiosaurus dinosaur, a reptile that lived 175 million years ago in Rutland. This skeleton proved to be one of the most complete sauropod dinosaurs ever found in Europe and one of the oldest of this family in the world. The rebuilt skeleton is now on display in the museum on New Walk in Leicester.

KETTON

Cattle being led down the Main Street, *c.* 1905, with The Blue Bell inn standing in the background and the village school to the right.

The limestone quarries, *c.* 1910. The brickworks are on the left.

Ketton Portland cement works in the 1940s. This company was formed in 1928, and the first kiln opened in 1929.

A view of the service line which connected the Ketton Portland cement works with the main line, 19 September 1956.

Seaton to Stamford Ivatt Class C12 4–4–2 leaving Ketton station, 7 October 1950. Ketton station opened on 1 May 1848, became Ketton and Collyweston station on 8 July 1935 and closed on 6 June 1966.

The packhorse bridge on the Ketton to Collyweston Road. Note the curved arches on the Rutland side and the pointed arches on the Northamptonshire side, as well as the different style of stonework on top of the centre cutwater. What a tale this bridge could tell of local government bureaucracy!

The small packhorse bridge and ford near the Church of St Mary, 1904 (vicar Revd Arthur Hillersdon Snowden, MA). This bridge was extensively altered and widened in 1849. The ford no longer exists because of the installation of a wooden footbridge.

Stone carving on the gravestone to William Hibbins, facing the footway near the parish church. The Hibbins family were local stonemasons.

LITTLE CASTERTON & TOLETHORPE

Little Casterton, 1904. The Engine Inn is on the right (landlord William Bagworth).

Boating on the River Gwash at Little Casterton, 1903. This mill pond was formed by the weir at Tolethorpe Hall.

An engraving of Tolethorpe Hall, 1684.

Tolethorpe water mill on the River Gwash, 1904. Edward Ridge was miller and baker; the water mill was working until 1957, crushing oats for horse and cattle feed. Tolethorpe Hall boat house is on the right.

PICKWORTH

The Pickworth arch at sunset. This is all that remains of the parish church of All Saints, built *c.* 1300 and destroyed in 1470 (see below).

Site of the Battle of Losecoat Field. In these fields on 12 March 1470 the Yorkists defeated the Lancastrians. At the height of the battle Sir Robert Welles and Sir Thomas Launde threw off their distinctive coats to avoid detection when they realized that all was lost. The victorious troops sacked Pickworth, destroying the parish church.

RYHALL

General view of the village on the north bank of the River Gwash, *c.* 1905. The photograph was taken from the bridge.

The village square, 1916. The Green Dragon public house is to the left of the photograph (landlord Tom Harry Woolley).

The Green Dragon public house, 1936 (landlord Walter Reginald Bennett). The Millstone public house is in the centre background (landlord Charles Horace Dearmer).

Foundry Road, looking east along the north bank of the River Gwash, *c.* 1914.

TICKENCOTE

The Main Street, Tickencote, *c.* 1910. The lych-gate to the parish church is on the right.

Tickencote Hall, 1904. Owned by Major John Maurice Wingfield of Market Overton, it was the home of the Dowager Marchioness of Exeter. This fine house was demolished in 1953.

The Norman chancel arch (*c.* 1160) in the Church of St Peter, 1904.

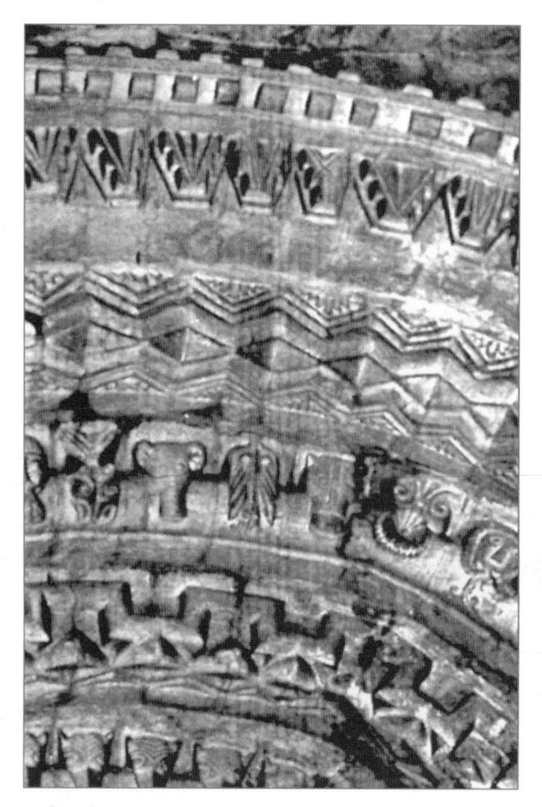

Left: The Norman stonemason's craft, as shown in a detail from the chancel arch. Right: The east end of the Church of St Peter, 1904 (vicar Revd Mordaunt Barton, BA). This church was almost completely rebuilt in 1792 at the expense of Elizabeth Wingfield.

TINWELL

The Main Street, 1936. The Crown public house is on the extreme right (landlord William Arthur Bellamy).

A general view of the village, looking east, *c.* 1905.

The Marquis of Exeter Harriers at Tinwell, 1904.

The blacksmith's forge with its stone horseshoe door surround. Established in 1848, for many years it was also the village post office. The stone horseshoe was obviously built on the instructions of a farrier, as it has eight nails.

ACKNOWLEDGEMENTS

The majority of the photographs and line illustrations printed in this book are from the author's own collection. Nigel Moon provided all of the windmill photographs. Philip Wells supplied mostof the photographs of the steam trains; he himself took these on his many visits to Rutland during the last fifty years. Rod Crowther of the *Rutland Times* allowed the author to select some of his photographs for inclusion in this book. Don Humberston provided the excellent fox-hunting scene on page 44. Justine Fosh of Ruddles Brewery was extremely helpful in providing photographs associated with the brewery at Langham. Thanks must be recorded to Neville Roberts and Geoffrey Turner of Castle Cement, Ketton. The author believes that all of the photographs that have been used from his collection are either out of copyright or they are his own personal property where copyright has been retained permission has been granted by the owner. Should this not be the case concerning some photographs he offers his sincere apologies and will make an acknowledgement in future editions. Finally, thanks are due to Angela Mallett for processing the manuscript for the publisher's use and to Gordon Williams who helped with the captions.

THE WOMEN'S LEGION TRAINING CENTRE:

The Cottesmore Hunt Kennels, Oakham, Rutland.

Students' Course four weeks, or longer if desired, in Agricultural and Horticultural Work. Fee, £1 a week for board, lodging and training; also a limited number of "loan trainings," fee payable in instalments of not less than 2s. a week when in situation.

For full particulars, apply—Miss Brocklebank, Commandant,
Wing Grange, Oakham.

The local branch of the Women's Legion, formed in 1915 by the Marchioness of Londonderry (see p. 21). It was run by Miss A.S. Brocklebank OBE, of Wing, at the Cottesmore Hunt Kennels near Ashwell. This postcard advertisement was issued during a recruitment drive in the First World War. The Women's Legion amalgamated with the Women's Army Auxiliary Corps in September 1917.

List of Places